THE

FLORAL KNITTING BOOK;

OR, THE

ART OF KNITTING

IMITATIONS OF NATURAL FLOWERS.

INVENTED BY A LADY.

British Library Cataloguing-in-Publication Data
A catalogue record for this book is available from the
British Library

Contents

Knitting

Knitting is a method by which thread or yarn is used to create a cloth. This knitted fabric will always consist of consecutive rows of loops, called stitches. As each row progresses, the knitter will pull a new loop through an existing loop, with the active stiches held on a needle – until another loop can be pasased through them. Knitting can be done by hand or machine, though most commonly it is a skilled craft created by hand – originally by country people with easy access to fibre. The word is derived from knot and ultimately from the Old English cnyttan, to knot. One of the earliest known examples of true knitting was cotton socks with stranded knit color patterns found in Egypt from the end of the first millennium AD. Initially a male-only occupation, the first knitting trade guild was started in Paris in 1527.

The process of knitting has three basic tasks:

The active (unsecured) stitches must be held so they don't drop.

These stitches must be released sometime after they are secured.

New bights of yarn must be passed through the fabric, usually through active stitches, thus securing them.

In very simple cases, knitting can be done without tools, using only the fingers to do these tasks; however, knitting is usually carried out using tools such as knitting needles, knitting machines or rigid frames. There are three basic types of knitting needles (also called 'knitting pins'). The first and most common type consists of two slender, straight sticks tapered to a point at one end, and with a knob at the other end to prevent stitches from slipping off. Such needles are usually 10–16 inches (250–410 mm) long but, due to the compressibility of knitted fabrics, may be used to knit pieces significantly wider. The most important property of needles is their diameter, which ranges from below 2 to 25 mm (roughly 1 inch). The diameter affects the size of stitches, which affects the gauge/tension of the knitting and the elasticity of the fabric. The yarn to be knitted is usually sold as balls or skeins, labelled as to its weight, length, dye lot, washing instructions – and suggested needle size. It is common practice amongst many knitters to keep these labels, for future reference if finishing / mending pieces.

Different types of yarns and needles may be used to achieve a plethora of knitted materials; these tools give the final piece a different colour, texture, weight, and/or integrity. Other factors that affect the end result include the needle's shape, thickness and malleability, as well as the yarn's fibre type, texture and twist. There are two major varieties of knitting: 'weft knitting' and 'warp knitting.' In the more common weft knitting, the wales (a sequence of stitches in which each stitch is suspended from the next) are perpendicular to the course of the yarn. In warp knitting, the wales and courses run roughly parallel, thus making them resistant to runs (commonly used in lingerie). In weft knitting, the entire fabric may be produced from a single yarn, by adding stitches to each wale in turn. By contrast, in warp knitting, one yarn is required for every wale. Since a typical piece of knitted fabric may have hundreds of wales, warp knitting is typically done by machine, whereas weft knitting is done by both hand and machine.

There are two further, important subdivisions in knitting: 'knit' and 'purl' stitches. In securing the previous stitch in a wale, the next stitch can pass through the previous loop from either below or above. If the former, the stitch is denoted as a knit stitch or a plain stitch; if the latter, as a purl stitch. The two stitches are related in that a knit stitch seen from one side of the fabric appears as a purl stitch on the other side. The two types of stitches have a different visual effect; the knit stitches look like 'V's stacked vertically, whereas the purl stitches look like a wavy horizontal line across the fabric. Patterns and pictures can be created in knitted fabrics by using knit and purl stitches as 'pixels'; however, such pixels are usually rectangular, rather than square, depending on the gauge/tension of the knitting. Individual stitches, or rows of stitches, may be made taller by drawing more yarn into the new loop (an elongated stitch), which is the basis for uneven knitting: a row of tall stitches may alternate with one or more rows of short stitches for an interesting visual effect.

Depending on the yarn and knitting pattern, knitted garments can stretch as much as 500%. For this reason, knitting was initially developed for garments that must be elastic or stretch in response to the wearer's motions, such as socks and hosiery. However, if they are not secured, the loops of a knitted course will come undone when their yarn is pulled; this is known as ripping out, unravelling knitting, or humorously, frogging (because you 'rip it', this sounds like a frog croaking: 'rib-bit'). To secure a stitch, at least one new loop is passed through it. Although the new stitch is itself unsecured ('active' or 'live'), it secures the stitch(es) suspended from it. To secure the initial stitches of a knitted fabric, a method for casting on is used; to secure the final stitches in a wale, one uses a method of binding/casting off. During knitting, the active stitches are secured mechanically, either from individual hooks (in knitting machines) or from a knitting needle or frame in hand-knitting.

Hand-knitting has gone into and out of fashion many times in the last two centuries, and at the turn of the twenty-first century it is now enjoying a revival. According to the industry group 'Craft Yarn Council of America', the number of women knitters in the United States age 25–35 increased 150% in the two years between 2002 and 2004. The latest incarnation is less about the 'make-do and mend' attitude of the 1940s and early 50s and more about making a statement about individuality as well as developing an innate sense of community. Additionally, many contemporary knitters have an interest in blogging about their knitting, patterns, and techniques, or joining a virtual community focused on knitting, such as the extremely popular 'Ravelry'. There are also a number of popular knitting podcasts, and various other knitting websites and knitting circles to join. We hope that the reader enjoys this book, and is encouraged to start some knitting of their own.

PREFACE.

ALTHOUGH the art of knitting has already produced almost innumerable articles, both useful and ornamental, the imitation of natural flowers by the knitting needle, has, it is believed, not yet been accomplished. Artificial-flower making would, probably, long ere this, have formed a favourite occupation in the drawing-room, but for the troublesome machinery required for their production.

No apology seems therefore necessary in introducing the present little work to the Public, as by following the simple rules here given, a few skeins of wool and a little wire, suffice to form accurate representations of natural flowers, which will be found an elegant and interesting amusement. As these flowers will bear washing when soiled, they not only form pretty ornaments for the room in vases, but from their durability, might be used for trimming ball dresses; the smaller kinds also, if knitted in silk, look well in bonnets or caps.

As the flowers here imitated are all copied from nature, should any doubt arise as to the exact shade of colour required, it would be well to take a natural flower to the shop, where the colour can be matched sufficiently near, to form an accurate representation. Berlin wool is used for these flowers, but it must always be split in two, unless the contrary is mentioned. This is very easily done, by first winding the skein round the fingers into a little ball; let this drop towards the ground; and, by taking two threads of the wool in each hand, it will be found to unwind itself very easily; wind it on cards, and it will be ready for use.

The white flowers look better, if washed before the wire is put in; warm soap-suds, with a little blue in it, does best for them—they must then be pressed in a clean cloth and dried quickly, either in the sun, or by the fire. The flowers themselves, when soiled, can be washed in the same way, and as the wire remains in, they must be pulled into proper shape when dry.

WHITE GARDEN LILY.

Six petals, six stamen, one pistil, are required to form each flower; two knitting-needles, No. 19, and a skein of superfine white Shetland wool.

Cast on four stitches.

First row.—Slip one, purl two, knit one.

Second row.—Make one, purl one, knit two, purl one.

Third row.—Make one, knit one, purl two, knit two.

Fourth row.—Make one, purl two, knit two, purl two.

Fifth row.—Make one, knit two, purl two, knit two, purl one.

Sixth row.—Make one, knit one, purl two, knit two, purl two, knit one.

Seventh row.—Make one, purl one, knit two, and purl two alternately to the end of the row.

Eighth row.—Make one, knit two, purl two alternately to the end of' row.

Ninth row.—Make one, purl two. knit two to end of row; knit last stitch plain.

Tenth row.—Make one, purl two, knit two to end of row; purl the last stitch.

Eleventh row.—Make one, knit one, knit and purl two alternately to the end of row.

You will now have fourteen stitches, making seven ribs; continue these seven ribs until you have knitted a length of three inches from the beginning of the work. Break off the wool, leaving a bit long enough to thread a rug needle with; with this needle take up seven stitches, which you must fasten off; then the other seven, and fasten in the same way, which completes one petal. Take a piece of fine wire sufficiently long to leave a small bit at the end for a stalk, and sew it neatly round the edge of the petal with white wool, which will make it in form.

Pistil.—Cut a length of wire of about eight inches, fold a bit of green Berlin wool in six, and split in two another bit of the same wool, place this lengthway with the other wool, and place the wire across the wool, fold the wire down, and twist it as tightly as possible, thus enclosing the wool; turn down the shortest end of the split wool, and twist the longest round it and the wire, so as to cover them evenly; fasten the wool with a slip knot at the end of the stem. Cut off a part of the green wool at the top, so as to leave merely a neat little tuft of wool at the end of the wire.

Stamens are made in the same way as the pistil, merely using yellow Berlin wool instead of green, and covering the stem with white instead of green. Place one stamen with every petal, twisting the wires of both together. The pistil is to be placed in the centre of the flowers when made up. Sew the petals together, leaving them open about an inch at the top, as neatly as possible, and draw them close at the bottom, twisting the stems together.

Buds.—Several buds are required; the large ones are of a very pale shade of green, the smaller ones of rather deeper colour. They look best in double knitting, and should be done in different sizes from twelve to twenty stitches. Knit about an inch of these different widths, and open them like a little bag. Take a piece of coarse wire, double some common wool about the thickness of your finger, put it across the wire, which must be folded down and twisted very tight; put this wool into the little bag, and gather the stitches of the bud at the top, catching the wire with your needle to fasten it. This will form the shape of the bud; fasten the stitches also at the bottom, and cover the stem with green wool split in two.

Leaves.—Different shades and sizes are required. Begin them all at the top, casting on four stitches; they look best in double knitting, without putting the wool twice round the needle; increase one stitch every second or third row, till you have eight stitches for the smallest, and sixteen for the largest size. Continue to knit without increase, till the leaf is the required length. The longest should be about a finger length, the smaller in proportion. The longest must be placed at the bottom of the stem when making up.

To finish a leaf, pull your needle out, and thread a rug needle with the wool, and pass it through the stitches so as to form a little bag, into which you must insert a bit of double wire; catch this at the top or sides to fix it, and it will keep the leaf in shape. Draw the wool *tight* on while the stitches are threaded, and twist the wool at bottom round the little stem.

The next operation consists in mounting the branch. Begin at the top with the smallest bud, round the stem of which some green wire must be twisted. Fix it at the top of a piece of bonnet wire, the length required for the long stem; continue to twist the wool round, and thus fasten the second bud, and the rest in the same way, at very small intervals. The flowers are fastened in a similar manner, according to taste, adding the leaves as needed.

Six buds, three flowers, and eight or ten leaves, form a beautiful branch.

Although the petals of the lily can be made up with the wool as it is, they look much better if, after being knitted, they are washed with a little blue in the water, and quickly dried, before the wire is put round them.

FUSCHIA.

If knitted in good size China silk, it does well to ornament caps or bonnets.

Calyx.—Four calyx are required for each flower; cast on eight stitches with crimson *split wool*.

First row.—Knit plain.

Second row.—Purl.

Third row.—Knit plain.

Fourth row.—Purl.

Fifth row.—Make one, knit two; repeat to the end of row.

Sixth row.—Purl.

Seventh row.—Knit plain.

Eighth row.—Purl.

Ninth row.—Knit plain.

Tenth row.—Purl.

Eleventh row.—Knit plain.

Twelfth row.—Purl.

Thirteenth row.—Make one, knit three; repeat to the end of row.

Fourteenth row.—Purl.

Fifteenth row.—Make one, knit four; repeat.

Sixteenth row.—Purl.

Seventeenth row.—Make one, knit five to the end of row.

Eighteenth row.—Knit six stitches, turn back and purl the same (leaving the rest of the stitches on the needle). Continue knitting and purling the six stitches until you have six small rows; then decrease one stitch, knit four; next row, decrease one, purl three, knit a row plain; then decrease one, purl two; lastly slip one, knit two together, turn the slipped stitch over, fasten the wool by putting it through the last stitch. This completes one division of the calyx. Break off the wool, leaving about a yard on the work, in order neatly to carry down the wool to the stitches, which are still on the needle. Then with the same wool, knit six more stitches, which must be done especially as the first, forming the second division, and with the same wool knit the third and fourth, which finishes the calyx.

Sew a bit of fine wire (with the same split wool) round the end of each division, and the ends of the wire must be sown two by two on the inside of the flower before it is sown up.

The corolla is small in the Fuschia, and less apparent than the calyx. The colour of the wool must be either purple or dark puce.

Cast on eight stitches.

First row.—Knit plain.

Second row.—Purl.

Third row.—Make one, knit two; repeat throughout the row.

Fourth row.—Purl.

Fifth row.—Knit plain.

Sixth row.—Purl.

Seventh row.—Make one, knit three; throughout tire row.

Eighth row.—Purl.

Ninth row.—Knit plain.

Tenth row.—Purl.

Eleventh row.—Knit four stitches, turn back, decrease one, purl two, and finish by slipping one, knitting two together, turning the slipped stitch over, and putting the wool through the loop; bring the wool down the edge in the same way as for the calyx, and knit the second, third, and fourth divisions like the first. Sew a bit of wire round the edge, following the simosities of the work, and sew the two edges together.

The pistil and stamen can be made like the lily, but very much finer and smaller; but a simpler and easier method is, to stiffen some pale green, or white sewing cotton, with gum, and cut eight pieces of it of about five or six inches long, for the stamen, and one bit rather longer for the pistil; tie them together, and dip the longest in gum, and then in some green powder, or wool cut as fine as powder, and the rest, first in gum, and then immediately in yellow powder, or wool cut as fine, which will answer quite as well for the purpose. Mount your flower, by placing the stamens and pistil inside the corolla, and that to within the calyx, sufficiently low to show the corolla slightly; sew the open side of the calyx, and twist all the stalks together, covering the little stem with green wool.

Buds.—Cast on four stitches, knit fine row plain, purl one row.

Third row.—Make one stitch, knit one throughout the row.

Fourth row.—Purl.

Fifth row.—Knit plain.

Sixth row.—Purl.

Seventh row.—Make one, knit two throughout the row.

Eighth row.—Purl.

Ninth row.—Knit plain.

Tenth row.—Furl.

Then gather all the stitches with a rug needle, make a little ball of red wool, put a bit of wire across it, fold over, and twist the wire quite tight, cover the little ball with the piece just knitted, sew the opening neatly, and gather up the stitches at the stem, which must be covered with crimson wool.

Leaf.—Cast on three stitches, knit, and purl alternate rows, increasing one stitch at the beginning of each row until the leaf is of the breadth desired (about seven stitches for the smallest, and fourteen or sixteen stitches for the largest); then knit and purl four rows without increase, and begin to decrease in every row, until you have but three stitches left, which knit as one, and fasten off. Sew a fine wire round the leaves, leaving a small bit at the end as a stalk, and also a fine wire doubled, at the back of the leaf, in the centre, which will keep it in shape.

Several shades and sizes of leaves are required, as also several buds and flowers, to form a handsome branch.

HEART'S-EASE.

This flower requires five petals to form it, two violet and three yellow; one of the latter must be larger than the rest, and of a deeper colour. All the wool must be split.

For the violet petals, cast on ten stitches on two needles, five on each; fold the two needles so as to bring the last stitch behind the first, and *double knit* a piece of rather more than half an inch in length, taking one stitch from one needle, and one from the other throughout each row. When you take the needles out, run the wool through them with a rug needle, and pass a piece of double wire through the little bag which the knitting has formed, catch it at the top and sides to keep it in form, draw up the other end, and twist the wires together after having shaped the wire to the form of the petal. The yellow petals are knitted in the same way, the largest requires twelve stitches, and the last four or six rows must be done with violet wool, to form the dark spot at the top. The two smaller yellow petals only require eight stitches, with two or four rows of violet at the top; twist the wires of the five petals together, and cover the stem with green wool; a cross stitch, like herring-bone, should be made with green wool, where the petals join in the middle of the flower.

For the calyx, thread a needle with whole green wool, fasten this on the stem, at the back of the flower, and take a herring stitch at the back of each petal, making the stitch rather long, and leaving the wool loose. The bud is formed by making a little tuft of yellow, violet, and green wool, mixed together; fix it on a piece of wire by crossing the wool over, and twisting the wire very tight, turn the ends of the wool down the wire, and fasten them at about a quarter of an inch down, by twisting some green split wool round, with which the little stein must be also covered.

Leaves.—Cast on three stitches.

Knit one row, purl one row, then

First row.—Make one, knit one throughout the row.

Second row.—Make one, purl the row.

Third row.—Make one, knit three, make one, knit one, make one, knit two.

Fourth row.—Make one, purl the row.

Fifth row.—Make one, knit five, make one, knit one, make one, knit six.

Sixth row.—Make one, purl the row.

Seventh row.—Cast off, or fasten off, three stitches, knit three, make one, knit one.

Eighth row.—Cast off three stitches, purl the row.

Ninth row.—Make one, knit five, make one, knit one, make one, knit four.

Tenth row.—Make one, purl the row.

Eleventh row.—Make one, knit seven, make one, knit one, make one, knit six.

Twelfth row.—Make one, purl the row.

Thirteenth row.—Fasten off three stitches, knit the remainder.

Fourteenth row.—Fasten off three stitches, purl the vest.

Fifteenth row.—Knit six, make one, knit one, make one, knit six.

Sixteenth row.—Purl the row.

Seventeenth row.—Knit seven, make one, knit one, make one, knit six.

Eighteenth row.—Purl the row.

Nineteenth row.—Fasten off three stitches, knit four, make one, knit one, make one, knit seven.

Twentieth row.—Cast off three stitches, purl the row.

Twenty-first row.—Knit six, make one, knit one, make one, knit five.

Twenty-second row.—Purl the row.

Twenty-third row.—Knit seven, make one, knit one, make one, knit six.

Twenty-fourth row.—Purl the row.

Twenty-fifth row.—Cast off three stitches, knit remainder.

Twenty-sixth row.—Cast off three stitches, purl remainder.

Twenty-seventh row.—Knit row plain.

Twenty-eighth row.—Purl the row plain.

Twenty-ninth row.—Knit row plain.

Thirtieth row.—Purl row plain.

Thirty-first row.—Cast off two, knit remainder.

Thirty-second row.—Cast off two, purl remainder.

Thirty-third row.—Knit row plain.

Thirth-fourth row.—Purl row.

Thirty-fifth row.—Knit row plain.

Thirty-sixth row.—Purl row plain.

Thirty-seventh row.—Cast off two, knit remainder.

Thirty-eighth row.—Cast off two, purl remainder.

Fasten oft the two last stitches.

It is on this principle that all kinds of indented leaves are made; by knitting more rows with increase between the castings off, they are made broader; by working more rows between the castings off, they are made longer; and by casting off more stitches at a time, the indentations are made deeper; so that the endless variety of natural leaves may be copied without difficulty.

Having completed the leaves, some wire must be sewn neatly round, following the turnings of the leaf exactly; and for the larger ones, it will be better to sew a double wire in the centre of the leaf at the back, which will conceal the openings left by the increase of stitches.

One or two flowers, with a bud, and two or three leaves, are sufficient for a small branch.

CONVOLVULUS.

Four needles are required.

Take some pale yellow split wool, and cast on six stitches on each of two needles, and three stitches on the third needle, knit two plain rounds.

Third round.—Knit one, make one, knife one, make one, knit two, make one, knit one, make one, knit two, make one, knit one, make one, knit two, make one, knit one, make one, knit two, make one, knit one, make one, knit one, knit two, plain rounds.

Sixth round.—Take a deeper shade of yellow; knit two, make one, knit one, make one, knit four, make one, knit one, make one, knit four, make one, knit one, make one, knit four, make one, knit one, make one, knit four, make one, knit one, make one, knit two, knit three plain rounds; take white wool and knit one more round.

Eleventh round.—Knit three, make one, knit one, make one, knit six, make one, knit one, make one, knit six, make one, knit one, make one, knit six, make one, knit one, make one, knit six, make one, knit one, make one, knit three, knit three plain rounds with white, then take pale blue (half twist silk may be introduced with good effect), knit one more plain round.

Fifteenth round.—Knit four, make one, knit one, make one, knit eight, make one, knit one, make one, knit eight, make one. knit one, make one, knit eight, make one, knit one, make one, knit eight, make one, knit one, make one, knit four. Take a deeper shade of blue, knit three plain rounds. Take a still deeper shade, and knit two rounds. Cast off very loosely.

The flower thus finished will be found divided into five stripes, by the increase stitches. Take a piece of wire, and sew it as neatly as possible along the edge of the top of the flower as far as the first stripe, turn down both ends of the wire. Take a second piece, and sew it from the first to the second stripe, turn down the ends, and contrive the same for the third, fourth, and fifth stripes. Sew down all the ends of wire two by two, on the wrong side of the flower. Sew up the side left open. The right side of the knitting will be the inside of the flower. Cover the lower end of the flower with fine herring-bone stitches to form a small calyx; tie up five bits of yellow wool not split with a knot at the top of each; fix them on a bit of wire to make the stamen, and place them in the centre of the flower, and cover the stem with green wool.

Buds.—Cast on four stitches in pale green wool.

First row.—Purl.

Second row.—Make one, knit one, repeat through the row.

Third row.—Purl.

Fourth row.—Knit plain.

Fifth row.—Purl.

Sixth row.—Make one, knit two, repeat through the row.

Seventh row.—Purl.

Eighth row.—Use two threads of blue wool, together with the two green, and knit the row, putting the wool twice round the needle. Gather all the stitches with a rug needle, then cut a small round of card, prick four holes in the centre, put two pieces of wire cross ways through the four holes, twist the wire tight under the card, and cover the little card with green or blue wool, as if winding it, Cover this with the knitted piece for the bud. Sew up the open side, gather together the stitches of the open part, and cover the stem with green wool.

Leaf.—Cast on three stitches.

First row.—Purl.

Second row.—Knit plain.

Third row.—Purl.

Fourth row.—Make one, knit rest of row plain.

Fifth row.—Make one, Purl the row.

Sixth row.—Knit plain.

Seventh row.—Purl row.

Eighth row.—Knit row.

Ninth row.—Purl row.

Tenth row.—Make one, knit rest of row.

Eleventh row.—Make one, purl rest of row.

Twelfth row.—Knit row.

Thirteenth row.—Purl row.

Fourteenth row.—Knit row.

Continue to knit and purl alternate rows, decreasing one stitch at the beginning of each, until only three stitches remain; knit these as one, and sew a fine wire neatly round the leaf, always leaving a little bit at the beginning and end as a stalk.

This will form a leaf of middling size, but a variety of sizes and shades of colour will be required to form a branch.

TIGER LILY; OR, TURK'S CAP.

Six petals for each flower; which must be knitted in bright orange wool, split in two.

Cast on four stitches. Knit and purl alternate rows, until you have done about an inch in length.* Continue knitting and purling, increasing one stitch at the beginning of each row, both plain and purled, until you have fourteen or sixteen stitches; then knit and purl alternately four rows more, without increasing; then continue to knit and purl, decreasing one at the beginning of each row, till three stitches only are left, purl these three as one, fasten the wool, and sew a piece of wire round the petal.

When the six petals are completed, take a needleful of dark red brown China sewing silk (or brown wool split in four) and embroider on each petal several long stitches, in imitation of the dark spots of the natural Tiger Lily.

Pistil.—Make a tuft of orange wool, with some brown wool mixed with it, fix it on a bit of wire, cut the wool quite short, and cover the stem with orange wool, split.

Stamen.—Take a piece of wire, call one extremity No. 1, and the other No. 2, begin in the middle of the wire to twist some brown wool, split in four, round the wire, going towards the extremity, No. 1; do the same with orange wool, beginning at the same point, but going towards No.

2. Having covered about the length of the nail of your little finger each way, fold the wire in the middle, and cover the remainder as the stem, with orange wool.

Mount the flower without sewing the petals together, as in the White Lily, but merely twist the six petals tightly together.

Buds and leaves are like those of the White Lily, but of a rather darker shade of green, the whole stem must be covered with green split wool.

<u>*</u> If the last row of four stitches is plain knitting, the first increasing row must be knit also, in order to turn the work, the right side becoming the wrong.

MICHAELMAS DAISY.

This flower may be knitted, with two stitches for the width of the row, but it is much quicker to work it in a chain of Crochet; it is generally variegated, either in two shades of red, or two shades of violet. The variegation is produced by working with two threads of Berlin wool, one of a deep, the other of a light shade, of the same colour.

Make a chain of simple crochet, about a yard in length, then cover a piece of thin wire, as long as you can conveniently manage, with one thread of Berlin wool, and begin to sew this wire along one edge of the chain, leaving about an inch of the wire at the beginning; when you have sewn about an inch, cut the chain, pull the thread through the last stitch, bring your wire round, sew half the second edge, then bring round the wire, that you left at the beginning, sew it to meet the other, letting the wires cross each other, twist them and the wool together tightly, to form a stalk, and turn up the two little petals, first cutting away one of the wires close to the twist, to prevent the stalk being too thick when finished.

Wind a piece of yellow wool on the end of one of your fingers, pull it out thus doubled, and twist a bit of rather strong wire over it, twist the wire very tight, and make with this wool a kind of little ball, which must be covered with a piece of common net (dyed yellow if possible), tie the net as tight as possible over the wool. This forms the Daisy.

When you have made a sufficient number of petals to form two or three rows, each row being made rather larger than the first, you must sew them all round the little heart, and proceed to make the calyx as follows:—

Make a chain of twelve stitches with the crochet needle, using green wool, not split, work two rows in double crochet, increasing two stitches in the second row. Sew this calyx under the petals, fasten up the open side, and gather the stitches of the lower extremity, cover the stem with green split wool.

Bud.—Make a small ball of any colour, then take fifteen or twenty bits of split wool, the same colours as used for the flower, each about an inch long, tie them tightly as a little bundle; fasten this on the top of the little ball, to which you must first fix a wire; bring down the ends of wool in alternate stripes of dark and light shades, tie all these ends round the wire, and cut them close. Wind a bit of green wool, as a very small ball, immediately under the bud, then with green wool, not split, make a row of herring-bone stitches, from the little bud, to about half-way up the coloured one. This makes a very pretty bud, looking as if just ready to bloom.

Leaf—like that of the Heart's-ease.

PINK GERANIUM.

Three or four flowers are required for a nice branch, with two leaves and five or six buds, some pink and some green.

Five petals must be made for each flower—two large; one middle-sized; and two small.

Two shades of pink split wool—one rather light; and the other deeper, for large petal.

Cast on two stitches, knit one row.

Second row.—Make one stitch, and purl the rest of row. Continue knitting and purling alternately, making one stitch before and after the middle stitch (still continuing to increase also at the beginning of each row) in the knitted row, until you have seventeen stitches; then take the darker shade, and knit and purl six rows, still increasing in the middle of the knitted rows, but decreasing one stitch at the beginning of every row, beginning the decrease in the same row in which you change the wool; then knit and purl alternately without increasing in the middle, and still decreasing one stitch at the beginning of each row, till you have but 9 stitches left. Cast these off. Sew a wire neatly round the petal with split pink wool, and one at the back also.

For middle-sized petal.

Cast on two stitches with a paler shade of pink wool, than used for the last petal.

Knit one row; make one stitch, purl the rest of row; knit one plain row, purl one row, and continue to knit and purl alternately, increasing* one stitch before and after the middle stitch in every other plain row, till you have eleven stitches.

Take the lightest shade used for the large petal, for the darkest of this, knit and purl alternately four rows, increasing in the middle of every plain row, and decreasing at the beginning of every row, then continue to knit and purl without increase in the middle, but decreasing at the beginning of each row, till but nine stitches remain; cast these off.

The small petals are made in exactly the same manner as the above, but increasing only to nine instead of eleven stitches, and casting off with seven stitches instead of nine.

LEAF.

Cast on ten stitches of a nice bright, but rather dark shade of green (a yellow green will be found to look most natural).

Knit one row.

Second row.—Make one, knit two, through rest of row. All the back rows arc purled, only increasing one at the beginning of each row, but not in the middle of the purled rows.

Third front row.—Make one, knit three, repeat through the row next front row; make one, knit four, through the row; continue to increase thus, till yon have about seven stitches between each increase. Then take a very dark shade of green, and knit and purl four rows without increase; join on the first colour again, and continue to increase as before, till you have eleven stitches between each increase, then begin to decrease by fastening off three stitches at the beginning of every third or fourth row, both in the knitted and purled rows, still continuing to increase in the centre, and thus decrease at the beginning till you have but five or six stitches, which fasten off in the usual way.

Sew a wire quite round the leaf, and also bits of double, up each of the divisions at the back of the leaf. The stitches must be taken deep enough to cover the holes left by the increasing.

Buds.—For the pink ones, take five or six bits of the different shades of pink wool, double them over a bit of wire, double the wire and twist it very tight; bring the ends of the wool down, and fasten them round the wire, about a quarter of an inch long or less, according to the size required; twist some; split green wool round the stem, and for the larger buds, make a few long herring-bone stitches in whole green wool, to form a little calyx.

The green buds are made in the same way, but rather smaller. They must be mounted on a piece of bonnet wire, the length required for a branch.

All the flowers placed at the top, the buds altogether round the stem, a little lower down, and the leaves still lower. Cover all the stems with green wool split.

<u>*</u> These stitches must not be incresed by bringing the wool forward, but by taking up a stitch and knitting it at the back; it does not make so large an opening as the usual way.

NARCISSUS.

One or two flowers only will be needed to form a branch, neither buds or leaves being required.

Six petals and three stamen for each flower.

Cast on one stitch in white split Berlin wool.

Second row.—Make one, and knit rest of row.

Third row.—Make one, purl the row.

Fourth row.—Knit plain row.

Fifth row.—Purl plain row.

Sixth row.—Make one, knit row.

Seventh row.—Make one, purl row.

Eighth row.—Knit plain row.

Ninth row.—Purl plain row.

Tenth row.—Make one, knit row.

Eleventh row.—Make one, purl row.

Twelfth row.—Knit row.

Thirteenth row.—Purl row.

Fourteenth row.—Make one, knit row.

Fifteenth row.—Make one, purl row.

You must now knit and purl alternately 10* rows without increase, and then begin to decrease one in the next knitted and purled rows; knit and purl one row plain; decrease one in the next two rows; knit two plain, and thus

34

continue till you have but three stitches left, gather these with a rug needle and fasten the wool.

The next most important part of this flower is the Nectarius, which looks like a little yellow cup, edged with scarlet.

The petals first made, must have a wire sewn neatly round them, and like all white flowers, will look better if washed and slightly blued, before the wire is put on.

FOR NECTARIUS.

Cast on six stitches in very pale yellow wool, split.

First row.—Knit plain.

Second row.—Purl.

Third row.—Make one, knit one, repeat through the row.

Fourth row.—Purl one row.

Fifth row.—Knit one row.

Sixth row.—Purl one row.

Seventh row.—Make one, knit two, repeat through the row.

Eighth row.—Purl one row.

Ninth row.—Knit one row.

Tenth row.—Purl one row.

Take scarlet wool (or scarlet China silk), knit one row, and cast off very loosely. Sew up the open side. Make a little tuft of pale green, or yellow wool, to fill the bottom of the little cup, and preserve its shape; place at the top of these, three stamen, each formed by a knot of yellow wool, fixed on a bit of wire. Then take green wool. Cast on six stitches; knit a piece about half an inch long, increasing irregularly about six stitches before you reach the top. Sew this piece under the flower, closing the open side.

The stem should be made of a piece of thin whalebone, about a quarter of an inch in width, which is better covered first, with a strip of green tissue paper, and then with green wool as usual; the flowers must be fixed to the top of this, according to their natural appearance.

* Seven stitches will be sufficient, if you make the flower double.

SCARLET GERANIUM.

Four flowers are required to form a branch, 2 leaves, and about five or six buds.

One double petal, and three small ones for each flower.

Double petal.

Cast on one stitch in white split wool, and continue to knit and purl alternately, increasing one at the beginning of each row, till you have seven stitches, knit one row, and purl one row plain; then fasten on a bright shade of scarlet wool, split, and continue to increase in each row, both knit and purled, till you have twelve stitches; you must then make one in the knitted wide, and after knitting six stitches only, turn back and purl them, leaving the other six stitches on the needle; continue to knit these six stitches, increasing one stitch on the right side, till you have ten stitches; knit one row, and purl one row without increase, and begin to decrease one in each knitted row till you have but five stitches left, then decrease one on each side till reduced to three stitches, which cast off.

The stitches which were left on the needle, must now be knitted in the same way, taking care that the increase and decrease be always in the purled, instead of the knitted rows, before, in order to form the heart-shape of the petal.

For small petals.

Cast on one stitch in white wool, and knit and purl alternate rows, increasing one stitch each row, till you have seven stitches, knit and purl one row plain, then fasten on scarlet wool, and continue to knit and purl alternate rows, increasing one at the beginning of each till you have eleven stitches, knit and purl four rows plain, and then begin to decrease in each row till yon have but three stitches left, which cast off.

One petal must be made of this size, and two smaller ones, exactly in the same way, only the stitches increased, must be to five instead of seven, and nine instead of eleven.

For stamen.

Take a bit of rather coarse reel cotton, five or six times doubled, and cross it over a piece of wire, which must be twisted very tightly, cut the thread about a quarter of an inch in length, after it is on the wire—this must be placed in the centre of the flower when mounted, and the wires twisted together.

The buds are made exactly like those of the pink geranium, only with scarlet wool, instead of pink.

The Leaf is also the same.

SNOW-DROP.

White silk half twist is the best material for this flower, but it can be done in white split Berlin wool.

Six petals are required for each snow-drop: three small ones in the interior of the flower, and three larger over these.

Cast on four stitches, knit and purl alternately six rows plain, knit and purl six more rows, increasing one stitch at the beginning of the first and second, the fifth and sixth rows, then knit and purl alternately eight rows without increase, and then begin to decrease one at the beginning of each row, till only four stitches remain; cast them off.

The small petals are knitted as three in one.

Cast on six stitches.

Purl one row, make one stitch, knit two, repeat through the row. All the back rows are purled. Make one stitch, knit three, repeat through the row; continue thus to increase at the beginning, and knit one stitch more each row between the increase, until you have seven stitches knitted between each, then purl one row, knit one plain row and purl another, after which, knit eight stitches, turn back and purl them, knit four stitches, purl them back. Break off your silk about a yard from the work, gather the four stitches together, and fasten them; thread a needle with the silk left, and take a stitch or two down the side of your work, till you bring the silk before the four remaining stitches, knit these, and purl them back; gather them together, and fasten as the last; bring the silk down to the next stitch, knit eight stitches, and proceed exactly as before with them, as also with the next. Sew a wire along the edge of the top with split wool, just as for the Fuschia. Embroider some little heart-shaped marks as in the natural flower, place the three exterior petals over these, and cover the stem with green, making it much thicker near the flower.

The buds must be made of silk or wool, as the flower. The smallest require eight or ten stitches to be cast on. Knit and purl a small piece, sufficient to cover a little bud of cotton wool, which must be fixed on a bit of wire, and covered with the piece just knitted.

The largest buds will require a few stitches to be increased, in order to make it wider at the top.

The leaves are very simple, the shape being much like blades of grass.

Cast on four stitches, and knit and purl alternate rows, till a sufficient length is done, gather the stitches at each extremity, and sew a fine wire neatly round.

CROWN IMPERIAL.

In order to form a pretty branch, four or five flowers must be made and placed round the stem, under a tuft of about twenty leaves. No buds are needed.

Six petals for each flower, which are knitted in one piece, as the Fuschia.

Cast on twelve stitches in scarlet split wool.

First row.—Knit plain.

Second row.—Purl plain.

Third row.—Make one, knit two, repeat through the row.

Fourth row.—Purl the row.

Fifth row.—Knit one row plain.

Sixth row.—Purl one row.

Seventh row.—Make one, knit three, repeat through the row.

Eighth row.—Purl one row.

Ninth row.—Knit one row.

Tenth row.—Purl one row.

Eleventh row.—Make one, knit four, repeat through the row.

Twelfth row.—Purl one row.

Thirteenth row.—Knit one row.

Fourteenth row.—Purl one row.

Fifteenth row.—Make one, knit five, repeat through the row.

Sixteenth row.—Purl one row.

Seventeenth row.—Knit one row.

Eighteenth row.—Purl one row.

Nineteenth row.—Make one, knit six, repeat through the row.

Twentieth row.—Purl one row.

Twenty-first row.—Knit one row.

Twenty-second row.—Purl one row.

Twenty-third row.—Make one, knit seven, repeat through the row.

Twenty-fourth row.—Purl one row.

Twenty-fifth row.—Knit one row.

Twenty-sixth row.—Purl one row.

Knit and purl alternately eighteen rows.

Then knit four stitches, make one, knit four, turn back, and purl the nine stitches just knitted, knit and purl the same alternately twice more, and continue to knit and purl, decreasing one stitch at the beginning of every row till but three stitches remain, gather these stitches together with a needle, and fasten them; break off your wool, and proceed in the same manner with the next eight stitches remaining on your needle; and thus continue till all the petals are completed. Sew a wire round the first division of the flower, then round the rest, and fasten all the wires inside, as for the Convolvulus.

Mak one pistil and six stamen exactly like those of the White Lily; fix them in the centre of the flowers by twisting all the stalks together, which must be covered with green wool, cutting away a few of the wires first, if found to be too thick. Sew up the open side of the flower.

The leaves are like those of the Lily, and must be made of different shades, the lightest at the top of the stem, the rest in rows round it. To mount the branch gracefully, it is better to knit as many of the largest sized leaves as you have flowers (each about a finger in length), place one flower to the stem, and immediately covering the stalk of the flower with the base of the leaf, and so on for each flower.

YELLOW JESSAMINE.

Four or five flowers for each branch. Five petals for each flower.

A pale, delicate shade of yellow looks best, and the wool must be split.

Cast on one stitch. Knit and purl alternately, increasing one stitch at the beginning of each row, till you have five stitches, then knit and purl alternately four rows without increase; continue to knit and purl, decreasing one stitch at the beginning of each row, till two stitches only remain, purl these two as one, and fasten off.

Sew a fine wire neatly round each petal, twist the five wires together closely, and cover them with split yellow wool for about the length of a quarter of an inch; cut off all the wires but two, and cover this little stalk with green wool.

Buds. Cover the middle of a bit of wire, by twisting one thread of yellow wool round it, put this wire across three or four pieces of yellow wool, split, fold the wire down, and twist it very tight, thus confining the wool in the middle; turn down the ends of yellow wool, and fasten them about a quarter of an inch down the wire, by twisting green wool round; cut the ends of yellow wool that remain, quite close, and cover the stem with the green wool.

The Jessamine leaves are generally placed in little branches of five in each branch, one larger at the top, the smaller ones placed on each side of the stem.

For top leaf.

Cast on three stitches.

First row.—Purl row.

Second row.—Knit plain.

Third row.—Purl row.

Fourth row.—Make one, knit one, purl one, knit one.

Fifth row.—Make one, purl the row.

Sixth row.—Make one, knit two, purl one, knit two.

Seventh row.—Make one, purl the row.

Eighth row.—Make one, knit three, purl one, knit three.

Ninth row.—Make one, purl the row.

Tenth, eleventh, twelfth, and thirteenth rows.—Knit and purl alternately, purling one stitch in the middle of each knitted row.

Fourteenth row.—Decrease one stitch, knit one, purl one, knit three.

Fifteenth row.—Decrease one stitch, purl the row.

Sixteenth row.—Decease one, purl one, knit two.

Seventeenth row.—Decrease one, purl the rest of row.

Eighteenth row.—Decrease one, knit the rest of row. Purl the two last stitches as one, and fasten off the wool.

The four smaller stitches must be made in the same way, but without the purled stitch in the middle, and beginning with one stitch instead of three, as for the larger. Sew a wire round each leaf, and mount them, covering all the steins with green wool.

Made in the USA
Columbia, SC
06 March 2019